SALISBURY
TO
WESTBURY

Vic Mitchell and Keith Smith

MP Middleton Press

First published December 1994

ISBN 1 873793 39 1

© Middleton Press 1994

Design - Deborah Goodridge

Published by Middleton Press
    Easebourne Lane
    Midhurst
    West Sussex
    GU29 9AZ
    Tel: (0730) 813169
(From 16 April 1995 - (01730) 813169)

Printed & bound by Biddles Ltd,
    Guildford and Kings Lynn

CONTENTS

ACKNOWLEDGEMENTS

In addition to the photographers shown in photographic credits, assistance has been received from R.M.Casserley, D.Clayton, G.Croughton, J.N.Faulkner, E.W.Fry, J.B. Horne, M.King, A.Ll.Lambert, N.Langridge, D.Lovett, J.Palm, J.S.Petley, Mrs E.Poynton, Mr.D.&Dr.S.Salter, the late N.Stanyon and our ever helpful wives. To all these we express our deep gratitude.

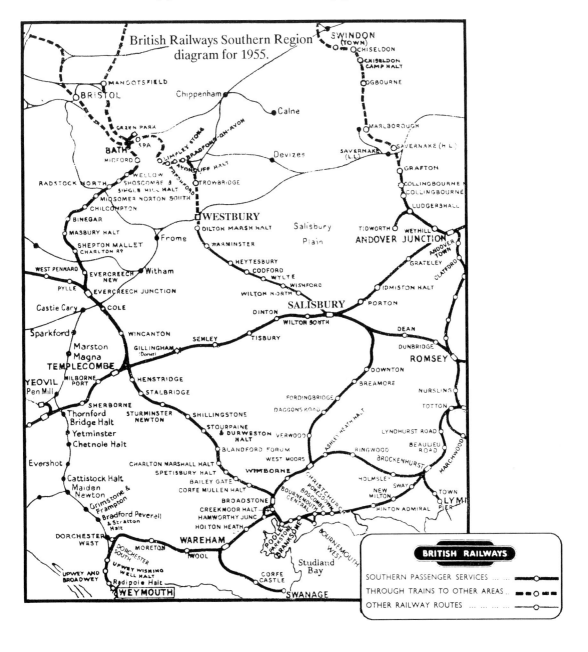

GEOGRAPHICAL SETTING

The route follows the valley of the River Nadder from Salisbury to Wilton and that of the River Wylye thereafter, nearly to Warminster. Most of the line thus far was built on the gravels of the floors of these valleys which cut deeply into the chalk of Salisbury Plain.

The steady climb ends almost two miles north of Warminster where the route crosses the watershed and falls steeply. It runs close to the Biss Brook, passing over outcrops of Upper Greensand and clay to reach Westbury. The maps are to the scale of 25" to 1 mile, unless shown to the contrary.

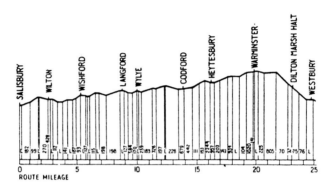

HISTORICAL BACKGROUND

The Wilts, Somerset & Weymouth Railway commenced services from the north to Westbury on 5th September 1848, opening the line from Thingley Junction that day. It continued west to Frome on 10th October 1850 and south to Warminster on 9th September 1851. Owing to financial difficulties, it became part of the Great Western Railway that year. The single broad gauge track was extended to Salisbury on 30th June 1856.

The London & South Western Railway reached Salisbury (Milford) in 1847 but its line through Salisbury Tunnel and the present station did not come into use until 1859.

The GWR progressively laid a third rail inside its broad gauge tracks to accommodate standard gauge trains to Salisbury. This took place on the Salisbury branch in June to August 1874. The last broad gauge train ran on the GWR in May 1892. The doubling of the route was completed in 1901, having been started in 1899.

GWR influence was all pervading, even after nationalisation in 1948 with the inclusion of the route in the Western Region. However, all stations south of Westbury were transferred to the Southern Region on 2nd April 1950 but the regional boundary was moved to a point four miles south of Warminster in 1980.

The GWR terminus at Salisbury was closed on 12th September 1932, all trains using the Southern Railway's platforms thereafter. The intermediate stations between Salisbury and Warminster were closed to passengers on 19th September 1955. The two pairs of double track between Salisbury and Wilton were reduced to one on 28th October 1973, when the former GWR lines were taken out of use.

Prior to the Railway Act of 1994, the route (together with the extension through Romsey) was allocated to Regional Railways, briefly known as Provincial Railways.

PASSENGER SERVICES

The table below indicates the down train (Westbury to Salisbury) frequency per day in selected years and reveals an overall steady improvement. Trains running on individual days of the week are not included; neither are the short workings south to Warminster that have operated in peak hours in many years of this century.

	Weekdays		Sundays	
	Fast	Slow	Fast	Slow
1870	-	4	-	1
1890	-	6	-	1
1910	3	8	-	2
1930	3	7	1	-
1950	4	6	4	-
1970	9	-	5	-
1980	10	-	7	-
1990	21	-	10	-

The Salisbury Railway & Market House Company was incorporated in 1856 and built a half-mile long branch to the town centre. It opened on 24th May 1859 and, being of standard gauge, was operated by the LSWR. While the facade still stands, this market hall has been replaced by the public library. The siding on the left is now the site of a public footway. More information is to be found in our *Basingstoke to Salisbury* album.

The most dramatic increase in recent years took place in May 1988 when the full Sprinter operated timetable was introduced. In May 1992, the weekday service was enhanced to 26 trains per day, the best ever.

Through running south of Salisbury began to appear in timetables around the turn of the century and gradually the number of trains so doing increased from two to four in the steam era. Subsequently, most trains ran to the South Coast.

Summer Saturdays brought an increase in through trains. For example, in 1955 there were nine to Portsmouth and two to Bournemouth via Wimborne. A weekday Cardiff to Brighton service was a feature of timetables in later years.

July 1908

WESTBURY and SALISBURY.—Great Western.

Miles.	Down.	Week Days.																Sundays.				
		mrn	mrn	mrn	mrn	h	mrn	aft	aft	aft	h	aft	aft	aft				mrn	aft	m		
	58 Cardiff ....dep.	....	....	6 40	7 46	10 10	1120	....	12 8	3 15	4 25	....	5 30	6 25	....	....	....	m	1 25	3 36	....	....
	32 Bristol (Temple Mds) "	m	6 0	8g10	10 5	11c22	1g0	m	2 25	4c25	5c33	6 5	7 35	8 45	....	....	....	8 35	3 45	6 30	....	....
—	Westbury ....dep.	6 16	7 20	9 32	1122	12 22	2 18	3 4	3 40	5 26	6 33	7 30	9 3	9 38	....	....	....	10 0	5 16	7 58	....	....
4¾	Warminster	6 27	7 35	9 47	1135	12 33	2 32	3 15	3 54	5 40	6 45	7 44	9 18	9 50	....	....	....	1013	5 30	8 12	....	....
8¼	Heytesbury		7 44	9 55	1143	....	2 39	....	4 1	5 47	....	7 52	9 26	d	....	....	....	1022	5 38	8 21	....	....
10¾	Codford	Except Mondays.	7 51	10 1	1149	....	2 45	....	4 7	5 53	....	7 58	9 32	d	....	....	....	1028	5 44	8 27	....	....
14¾	Wylye...........		8 0	1010	1158	....	2 52	....	4 15	6 1	....	8 7	9 41	d	....	....	....	1038	5 52	8 37	....	....
19¼	Wishford...........		8 10	1018	12 7	....	3 0	....	4 23	6 9	....	8 16	9 49	d	....	....	....	1047	6 1	8 46	....	....
22	Wilton*		8 18	1023	1214	....	3 6	....	4 30	6 16	....	8 23	9 56	d	....	....	....	1054	6 8	8 52	....	....
24½	Salisbury 112, 115, 118 ar		8 25	1035	1221	1 5	3 15	....	4 37	6 23	7 17	8 30	10 3	1025	....	....	....	11 0	6 15	9 0	....	....
49¾	115 Southampton †....arr.		9‡46	1213	1 44	1‡58	4‡35	....	6 48	7‡39	8‡6	1023	12 7	12 7	....	....	....	2‡57	8 25	....	....	....
69½	115 Portsmouth Town "		11 2	1251	2 23	2 59	4 50	....	....	8 16	9 17	1125	1245	1245	....	....	....	4 1	8 39	....	....	....

Miles.	Up.	Week Days.														Sundays.				
		mrn	mrn (Mondays only.)	mrn (Mondays only.)	mrn	mrn	n	mrn	mrn	aft	aft	aft	aft	n	aft		mrn	mrn	m		
	112 Portsmouth Town dep.	1220	m	....	....	6 5	8 7	....	9 50	b	1225	2b32	....	5 0	5 42	....	1220	....	12 0	....	....
	112 Southampton †.... "	1 0	....	....	....	6 45	9‡14	....	11‡6	....	1‡40	3‡32	....	6‡4	6 20	....	1 0	....	1242	....	....
—	Salisbury ....dep.	2 35	5 55	....	7 45	9 15	10a10	1030	1 5	....	2 35	4a25	5 0	6a52	7 45	....	2 35	8 20	4 0	....	....
2¼	Wilton*		6 2	....	7 53	9 23	....	1039	1 13	....	2 44	....	5 8	....	7 54	....	....	8 28	4 7	....	....
5¼	Wishford...........		6 8	....	7 59	9 29	....	1045	1 19	....	2 51	....	5 14	....	8 0	....	....	8 34	4 13	....	....
9¾	Wylye...........	Except Mons.	6 18	....	8 9	9 39	....	1056	1 29	....	3 4	....	5 25	....	8 11	....	....	8 44	4 23	....	....
13¾	Codford		6 27	....	8 17	9 48	....	11 5	1 37	....	3 13	....	5 34	....	8 19	....	....	8 52	4 32	....	....
16	Heytesbury		6 33	m	8 25	9 55	....	1112	1 44	m	3 22	....	5 41	....	8 27	....	....	8 59	4 38	....	....
19¾	Warminster...........	3 5	6 43	6 43	8 35	10 7	....	1123	1 55	3 20	3 35	4 58	5 52	7 32	8 38	....	3 5	9 10	4 49	....	....
24½	Westbury 32, 35 ....arr.	o	6 53	6 53	8 44	1017	10 50	1132	2 3	3 30	3 48	5 7	6 2	....	8 47	....	o	9 19	4 58	....	....
52¾	36 Bristol (Temple Mds) ar	4 13	8 17	8 17	10 4	1139	11c50	1 41	3 33	4k45	5 7	6 10	7 27	8c43	1010	....	4 13	1040	6 55	....	....
90¾	54 Cardiff........... "	7 28	1014	1014	1231	....	12 56	3 41	5 53	....	7 1	8 3	9 15	9 55	12 2	....	1025	3 25	8 13	....	....

a L. & S. W. Station.
b Through Trains, Portsmouth to Bristol,
c Stapleton Road.
d Stops to set down from Melksham and beyond, or Frome and beyond on informing Guard at Westbury.
g Through Trains, Bristol to Portsmouth,
h Through Express Trains from Cardiff to Southampton and Portsmouth,
k Commences on the 11th instant.
m Motor Car, one class only.
n Through Trains from Portsmouth and Southampton to Cardiff,
o Stops to set down from L.& S.W. Line on informing Guard at Salisbury.
* Over ¼ mile to L. & S. W. Station.
† Town and Dock Station.
‡ Southampton West.

SALISBURY

1. As at Basingstoke, the GWR branch terminus was provided with complete weather protection by means of a timber-built shed but here the trusses are of iron. Both had smoke hoods over the arrival road. (British Rail)

The GWR station is marked "Terminus" on this 1879 survey. Below it is the LSWR's down platform (with bay), their separate station for up trains being to the right. The Market House branch is lower right. The lines on the left are (from top to bottom) - GWR single track to Westbury, GWR siding, LSWR siding, LSWR double track West of England main line with a refuge siding below it. The goods shed in the centre of this page had been the "Transfer Shed" where broad and standard gauge wagons stood on opposite sides of a central platform.

→

3. The office building at the east end of the shed is now a listed structure and is in commericial use. It is seen here serving its original purpose and prior to the loss of its canopy. On the left is the footbridge which was erected in 1860 to link the GWR station with the LSWR platforms. It was demolished in 1956. (British Rail)

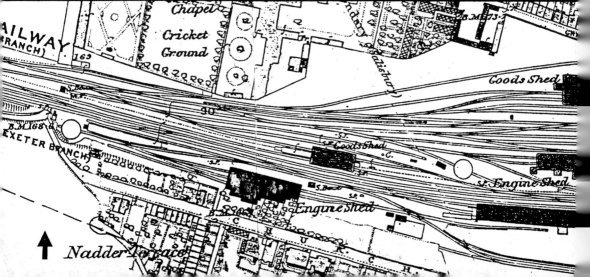

2. The enclosed structure would have kept out all but the prevailing west winds. The two centre roads seemed to have been used for stock berthing but may have originally been connected to the other two by means of wagon turntables and a transverse line. (British Rail)

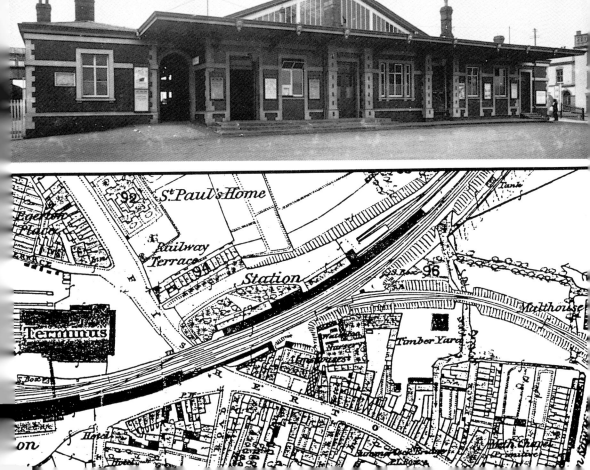

4. This eastward view of the GWR's first engine shed here has part of the LSWR's original station on the right. The former was closed in 1899 to allow for the expansion of the latter from one to four through parallel platforms. (British Rail)

5. A closer view of the original engine shed features the sand drier in the foreground and the connecting footbridge in the background. In the last year of the GWR (1947), the Salisbury allocation was two Hall class 4-6-0s and one 0-6-0PT. (British Rail)

Salisbury	1903	1913	1923	1933
No. of passenger tickets issued	55779	50710	39352	18816
No. of season tickets issued	-	-	54	5
No. of parcels forwarded	30316	37608	69548	18816
General goods forwarded (tons)	6795	5809	4973	2086
Coal, Coke etc. received (tons)	6790	8085	7897	16680
Other minerals received (tons)	3296	3796	3223	16462
General goods received (tons)	10354	12529	11790	15562
Trucks livestock forwarded	879	1122	690	564

6. A westward view from the up platform reveals that this was the only one signalled for the departure of passenger trains. One siding retains some of the original "baulk road" - longitudinal timbers with tie bars. The down platform had been extended in 1916. (British Rail)

7. Moving beyond the end of the up platform we see the double track connection running diagonally between the GWR and the LSWR, the latter's West Box being in line with the signal. This photograph was taken from the signal box seen in pictures 14 and 15. (British Rail)

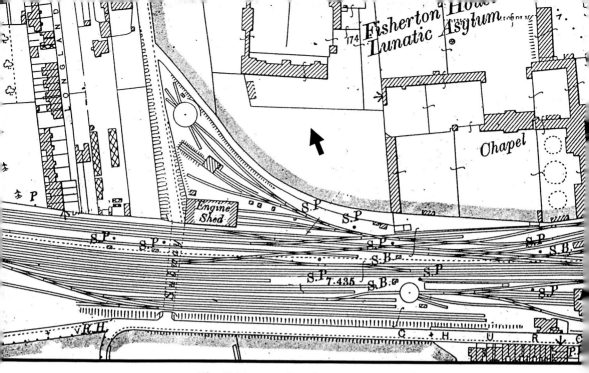

The 1901 survey has the two LSWR engine
sheds near the centre of the map and that of
the GWR on the left. The GWR's terminus
and goods shed are on the right.

8. Further west was the second engine shed, which had three roads instead of two. One siding separates it from the running lines. Smoke appears to be rising from the coal stage - more probably it is from the coalman's lobby. (British Rail)

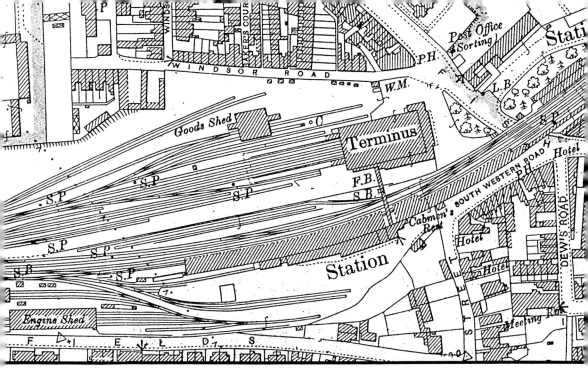

9. With cattle wagons in the GWR yard, a GWR 4-4-0 hauls a clerestory coach through the LSWR's platform 3. This may be a through coach for attachment to or detachment from an LSWR train. Visible are two of that company's pneumatically operated signals. (Lens of Sutton)

10. The 12-ton capacity goods yard crane, bridge rails and a horse box are all to be seen from the up platform of the GWR station which was closed to passengers on 12th September 1932. (Lens of Sutton)

11. No. 5925 *Eastcote Hall* worked the 10.15am Portsmouth & Southsea to Bristol Temple Meads on Sunday 21st August 1949. The train was too long for platform 3 and so the locomotive is standing beyond the starting signals. On the ground is the pneumatic equipment for the points. (J.H.Aston)

12. The ex-GWR engine shed closed on 26th November 1950 and was photographed on 21st May 1957. Centre is the water column and sand drier, while on the right is a typical GWR coaling plant (one is still to be seen at the Didcot Railway Centre). Coal wagons were propelled up an inclined siding, which was once situated on the grass covered bank, and unloaded under the shelter. The coal was stored under the water tank and discharged from the projecting shelter into a locomotive standing on the siding. This continued on to the 65ft turntable which was removed on 17th August 1958, although still used at busy times in 1956. At that time the shed housed preserved ex-LSWR 4-4-0 class T3 no. 563 and Terrier 0-6-0T *Boxhill*. (H.C.Casserley)

13. This and the next two pictures were taken after light snowfall in December 1965. A view towards the old terminus shows that the overall roof had gone but that the ex-GWR goods shed was still in use. On the right are the three end-loading docks and the water tank. (J.J.Smith)

14. Looking west from the brake van shown in the previous picture, we see "C" Box and the wall behind platform 1. The van on the left is on the approximate position of the first engine shed. In the distance is the 1926 flat-roofed West Box, by then "B" Box. (J.J.Smith)

15. This is the south elevation of "C" Box which was so annotated on 5th November 1950. It was opened on 28th May 1900 and closed on 28th October 1973 but continued in use as a ground frame for five weeks for traffic to Quidhampton sidings, prior to the opening of new connections at Wilton Junction. (J.J.Smith)

16. The interior of "C" Box was photographed on 16th September 1972 with the new track diagram taped over prior to its introduction two weeks later when the Quidhampton sidings came into use. By this date only 65 of the 95 levers were required. (G.Gillham)

17. Type 3 Hymek no. D7031 was recorded at platform 3 with the 13.23 Saturdays only Portsmouth Harbour to Swansea service in July 1968. The building behind it originally supplied hot-water-filled foot warmers to passengers and has more recently been used by carriage and wagon examiners. (D.J.Aston)

18. With the ex-GWR goods shed on the left, class 52 Western diesel-hydraulic no. D1043 *Western Duke* passes platform 3 on 20th May 1972 with stone wagons returning empty from Merstham to Merehead Quarry in Somerset. (G.Gillham)

19. The pneumatic cylinders are visible on the signals in both this and the previous picture. The 11.14 Bristol to Portsmouth Harbour is approaching Salisbury on the old LSWR up main line on 27th June 1981, hauled by nos. 31263 and 31286. Both distant signals here were fixed at caution due to the severe speed restriction through the station. (G.Gillham)

20. A class 25 locomotive was unusual on a Southern Region passenger service in 1983. No. 25069 stands at platform 4 with the 12.10 Portsmouth Harbour to Cardiff on 19th September 1983 with Mk.I coaches in tow. (C.Hall)

21. The white building lower left is the original LSWR station and the white wall attached to it is that of the bay platform (no. 6). To the right of this are the former GWR terminal buildings. Above them and between the white painted exhibition coaches are coal staithes, supplied by road. Industrial premises occupy a wedge-shaped plot of land that was once the GWR locomotive depot. Nearby are sidings which formed part of the GWR main line until 1973, when most of the ex-LSWR West Yard sidings were removed. (R.C.H.Poynton)

22. A firm of mobile exhibition organisers moved from Wimborne to the former GWR site in 1975. Earlier known as TrainEx, they became Rail Ambassador Ltd and undertook some specialised coach maintenance work for BR, such as the internal refitting of Mk.I charter coaches. FK13318 is outside the former goods shed on 9th April 1989. (G.Gillham)

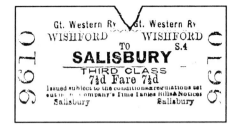

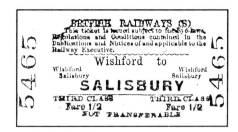

←

23. The then-new class 155 "Super-sprinter" units took over all services on the Salisbury-Bristol route from the class 33s in May 1988. All were withdrawn from service with door problems the following December and not fully reinstated until August 1989. They were finally replaced on the route by class 158 "Sprinter Express" units during March 1991 and all were subsequently converted into single unit railcars. No. 155311 is working the 13.10 Portsmouth Harbour to Cardiff service on 24th August 1989, some exhibition coaches being visible behind the second coach. (G.Gillham)

24. The exhibition trains moved away in 1991 to vacate the site for the construction of a traincare depot for the new fleet of class 159 DMUs for the Waterloo-Exeter route. This is the state of progress on 11th April 1992, the builder being Osborne of Chichester. (M.Turvey)

Other views and maps of this station can be found in the companion albums Branch Lines around Wimborne, Basingstoke to Salisbury, Salisbury to Yeovil **and** Fareham to Salisbury.

25. Two of the 3-car class 159 air-conditioned sets are seen from the end of platform 4. Beyond them is the toilet discharge siding and the carriage washing plant. Initially there was trouble with neighbours over noise at night but this was resolved by the erection of a high wooden fence. (M.Turvey)

26. The historic and novel pneumatic signalling was abandoned in August 1981 in favour of standard colour light signals controlled from a panel in the former parcel room of the original LSWR station. Class 159s stand at platform 1 on 6th May 1993, the line being restricted to use by freight and empty trains. Hampshire DEMUs (right) would not be seen in the area much longer. (C.L.Caddy)

27. The maintenance depot which cares for the entire 159 fleet, includes lifting and chassis cleaning facilities, less necessary now that modern trains have toilet retention tanks. This August 1993 view shows that platform 1 is devoid of sign boards. (V.Mitchell)

WEST OF SALISBURY

28. The summer of 1964 was to be the last for steam-haulage of passenger workings on the Bristol-Salisbury route, and was restricted to a number of Saturdays-only diagrams. One such was the 13.42 Bristol-Portsmouth, seen here running through the outskirts of Salisbury behind Grange class 4-6-0 No. 6874 *Haughton Grange* on 25th July. Houses now stand here. (G.Gillham)

29. On 25th April 1973, green-liveried class 47 no. 1613 (later 47033) climbs away from Salisbury with the 17.25 Portsmouth-Cardiff. To the right of the train a rake of empty freight-liner flats are stabled in the exchange siding, the exit points from which were worked by a small ground frame released electrically from Salisbury "C" Box. (G.Gillham)

30. Following the successful introduction of the five class 59 General Motors type 5 locomotives by Foster Yeoman Ltd for stone haulage from Merehead Quarry in 1986, rival firm Amey Roadstone Co. (ARC) followed suit with a further four class 59s of their own in 1990. One of these, no. 59101 *Village of Whatley* leaves Salisbury on the former LSWR route with the 14.39 Fareham - Whatley Quarry empty hoppers on 5th May 1993. (G.Gillham)

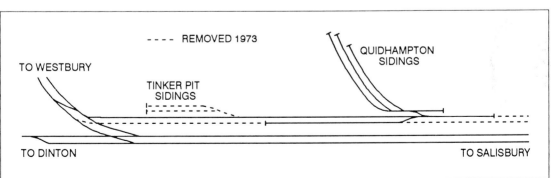

Diagram of Quidhampton Sidings and
Wilton Junction since 1973.

31. The connection from the ex-GWR Wilton-Salisbury line to the English China Clay Ltd quarry and works at Quidhampton was installed in 1972, initially for local transfer workings from the rail-served chalk pit at East Grimstead, between Salisbury and Dean. By the mid-1980s however, chalk slurry was being exported from Quidhampton to paper manufacturers in both Kent and Scotland - initially via the Speedlink network but latterly by dedicated block trains. In this view on 25th March 1991, no. 47445 shunts loaded tanks on the former main line, with the quarry entrance to the right. Further west, two sidings at Tinkerpit were in use by the Anglo American Oil Company from 1939 until 1973. (G.Gillham)

32. Lacking any name or identifying number, English China Clay Ltd 0-4-0 diesel-hydraulic shunter draws a rake of loaded slurry tanks out of the quarry on 29th May 1990. They would then be left on the former main line in the foreground for later collection by a BR locomotive and transfer to Eastleigh to form part of a Speedlink working to Scotland. (G.Gillham)

33. The three sidings were well filled when recorded on 7th July 1993. In addition to its use in paper manufacture, much of the chalk (calcium carbonate) is used in the paint, plastic and rubber industries. (V.Mitchell)

34. No. 33056 *The Burma Star* and no. 33059 pass Wilton Junction, with the 06.15 Three Bridges - Meldon Quarry empties on 31st May 1988. The train would have to reverse at Westbury and Exeter. The track in the foreground is the ex-LSWR route to Yeovil, and the crossover for traffic to the Quidhampton Sidings is in front of the first locomotive. (G.Gillham)

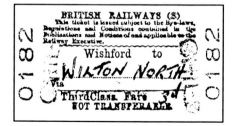

35. The parting of the ways near Wilton is seen on 16th February 1969 as class 35 Hymek no. D7070 works the 11.23 Portsmouth-Cardiff and on the right Warship class 42 no. D806 *Cambrian* slows the 11.10 Waterloo - Exeter for the approaching single line section. Such a scene has been impossible since 28th October 1973 when the two routes were joined at the new Wilton Junction just behind the bridge. (G.Gillham)

WILTON NORTH

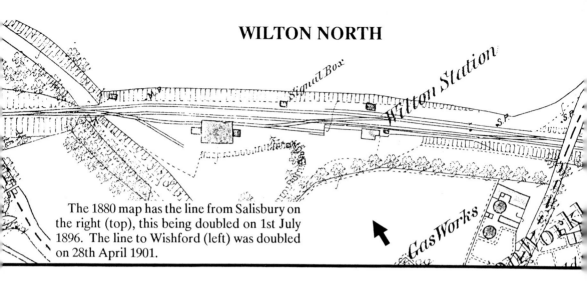

The 1880 map has the line from Salisbury on the right (top), this being doubled on 1st July 1896. The line to Wishford (left) was doubled on 28th April 1901.

36. The LSWR coaches suggest that this is a through train to Portsmouth. No. 3208 is a class 3206 or "Barnum" 2-4-0 of 1889, designed by Mr Dean with sandwich frames. Although probably laid at the time of the doubling, the long refuge siding on the right has longitudinal timbers. (British Rail)

The 1925 survey shows the proximity of the SR Wilton station (lower). The suffixes "North" and "South" were not applied until 26th September 1949. The population of this historic market town ranged from only 1800 to 2800 during the life of the station. Historically important, the town gave its name to the county, its borough status becoming that of a metropolitan borough in 1885. The 1855 gasworks (centre) was purchased by the corporation in 1888, its main customers being the famous carpet factories. It was sold to the Salisbury Gas Company in 1929 and closed soon after. Until then it required about 950 tons of coal per annum, most of which would have been carted along the direct roadway from the GWR yard.

Goods Shed

W.M^{co}

S.R.

B.B.

S.P.

S.P.

Wilton Station

193

192

Poor Law Institution
(Kingsway House)

Chapel

Gas Works
(Wilton Corp.)

S.Ps

C.R.

Allotmen

S.P.

3 ft.Tk.H.

W.M.

Wilton Station
F.B.

L.B.

S.B.

S.P.

Fairfield Cottages

S.P.

Goods Shed

Cattle Pens

F.F.

S.P.

Muni.Boro.Bdy.

M.P.

Burden's Ball Farm

Fair Field

Whiting Work

37. The complex pointwork at the north end of the station was photographed on 17th September 1955, the last day of passenger service here. By then the lamp room seen close to the footbridge in the previous picture had vanished. (E.Wilmshurst)

Wilton	1903	1913	1923	1933
No of passenger tickets issued	22994	14268	4956	865
No. of season tickets issued	-	-	19	3
No. of parcels forwarded	3369	3978	4646	5016
General goods forwarded (tons)	1551	4625	3985	3263
Coal, Coke etc received (tons)	1983	1021	1878	1149
Other minerals received (tons)	1116	321	545	1328
General goods received (tons)	1028	1273	1360	1451
Trucks livestock forwarded	175	193	202	157

38. Recorded soon after closure, the buildings and footbridge did not remain standing for long. The sidings and crossover were removed in May 1968. (A.W.Burges)

39. The goods yard remained open until 6th September 1965. Coal wagons are visible on the left of this photograph from July 1963. Southern Region influence is evident in the form of a signal post built from running rails. There was an up refuge siding behind the camera until 1954 - see the 1925 map. (H.C.Casserley)

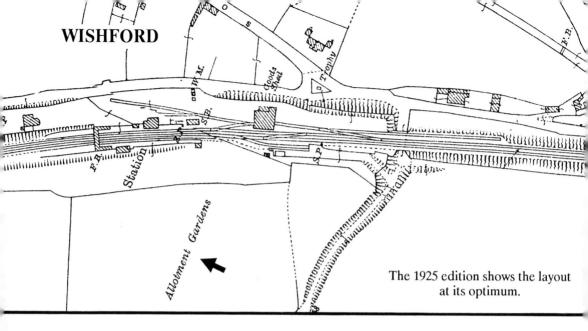

WISHFORD

Goods Shed

Trophy

Station

Allotment Gardens

The 1925 edition shows the layout
at its optimum.

Wishford	1903	1913	1923	1933
No of passenger tickets issued	12340	10943	8102	3994
No. of season tickets issued	-	-	55	34
No. of parcels forwarded	2732	4737	7272	3972
General goods forwarded (tons)	1694	1802	2384	432
Coal, Coke etc received (tons)	939	850	217	129
Other minerals received (tons)	1138	1103	791	1168
General goods received (tons)	3339	2899	2560	1112
Trucks livestock forwarded	28	86	95	88

40. The station was situated on a 31-chain curve where the route assumes a more westerly orientation towards Warminster. A train from that direction is approaching the down platform. (Lens of Sutton)

41. The line to Wilton (direction of view) was doubled on 28th April 1901 and that to Wylye was completed on 3rd March 1901. The covered footbridge was provided at about that time. (Lens of Sutton)

42. The cattle dock (right of centre) was added in July 1909. In the background is a good view of the surrounding chalk uplands. Passenger and freight facilities were both withdrawn on 19th September 1955. (Lens of Sutton)

43. The 1901 signal box remained in use until about 1968 but the sidings were lifted in 1961. On the left is the lamp room, in the usual position for such potentially inflammable structures - remote from other buildings. (Lens of Sutton)

44. Station House, visible in the previous picture, was still standing in 1993. The population of Great Wishford dropped from 378 in 1851 to 234 in 1951 - hence the poor traffic figures. (V.Mitchell)

WEST OF WISHFORD

45. No. 35028 *Clan Line* was photographed on 27th April 1974 working a return trip between Basingstoke and Westbury, its first outing since preservation. The train had been hauled from Waterloo by electric locomotive no. 74004. (A.G.Thorpe)

46. On several occasions over the years 1980-83, extensive engineering work closed much of the Western Region West of England main line on Sundays and the first few trains in each direction had to be diverted via the circuitous route of Swindon, Chippenham, Melksham, Westbury, Salisbury (reverse) and Yeovil to Exeter. This brought High Speed Trains to Salisbury for the first time, and here, on 12th October 1980, set no. 253001 heads down the Wylye Valley near Langford with the 08.14 Paddington - Plymouth. (G.Gillham)

47. The winter sun casts long shadows across the Wylye valley on 26th November 1986 as snowplough-fitted no. 47106 heads the 09.07 Eastleigh-Severn Tunnel Junction Speedlink service north of Wishford. Apart from five covered vans, the train consists of chalk slurry tanks from Quidhampton and, at the rear, eight empty coal hoppers from Totton, near Southampton. Six months later all Speedlink services ceased using this route, being diverted via Reading and Swindon. (G.Gillham)

48. No. 47106 passes the church of St. Nicholas at Little Langford on 6th September 1986 with empty MSV wagons from the ARC stone terminal at Fareham. Grazing cattle enhance the scene. (C.Wilson)

49. Only railway passengers and those using the minor roads can enjoy the scenic and architectural joys of the Wylye Valley to the full. Sprinter no. 158829 speeds past Little Langford on 7th July 1993 working the 10.30 Cardiff to Portsmouth Harbour. (V.Mitchell)

50. With a logo for the myopic and blue livery, no. 56049 passes Hanging Langford on 22nd July 1986 with 09.55 Ardingly - Westbury ARC empties. This village had 634 inhabitants in 1851 and Little Langford had 38. Despite the total being comparable with other villages on the line, Langford station was closed in October 1857. It had no sidings. (C.Wilson)

51. No. 59001 *Yeoman Endeavour* roars east with the 12.40 Merehead Quarry to Eastleigh Aggregate Terminal on 22nd July 1986. The bell below the horns of the locomotive had been presented by the locomotive's manufacturer (General Motors) at the naming ceremony on 28th June 1986. (C.Wilson)

52. On many occasions during the 1980s, engineering work on the single line sections west of Salisbury meant that all Waterloo - Exeter services had to be diverted via Westbury and Yeovil Pen Mill. On 4th November 1984 no. 50037 *Illustrious* is seen east of Wylye with the 09.45 Exeter to Waterloo. (G.Gillham)

53. A pair of class 119 DMUs, with set no. P581 leading, is seen at Hanging Langford, east of Wylye, forming the 12.56 Portsmouth - Bristol service on 15th August 1974. At this time these units were sharing the bulk of the passenger workings on this route with the Southern Region's Hampshire units. (G.Gillham)

WYLYE

54. Originally spelt "Wiley", the name was changed in August 1874 but the pronunciation remained unaltered. Doubling in this direction took place on 3rd March 1901 and in the other on 13th January 1900. (Lens of Sutton)

The 1939 survey has the up refuge siding right (lower) and the down one on the left (upper). The population dropped from 510 to 400 during the period of passenger service.

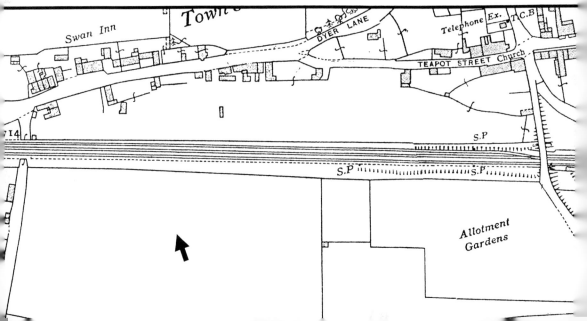

55. Elegant topiary on the down side contrasts with a cast iron urinal on the up platform. The post on the left was for a pressurised oil lamp, the simple wick type having been superseded generally after World War II. By 1994, the only trace of the station was the base of the signal box. (Lens of Sutton)

Wylye	1903	1913	1923	1933
No of passenger tickets issued	11483	10859	9529	5314
No. of season tickets issued	-	-	41	29
No. of parcels forwarded	8591	11816	13117	3006
General goods forwarded (tons)	1755	1555	1556	241
Coal, Coke etc received (tons)	742	867	283	278
Other minerals received (tons)	420	308	476	384
General goods received (tons)	2284	2829	3267	1748
Trucks livestock forwarded	168	164	76	75

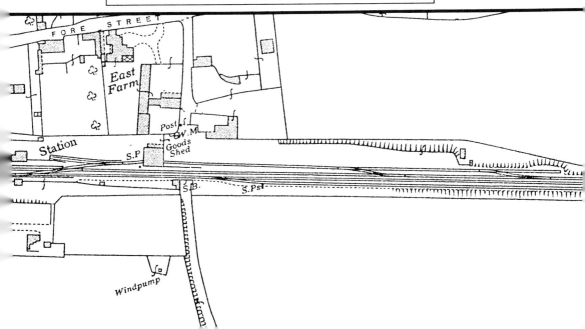

56. A light engine is approaching the lamp room, having just passed over the level crossing. The signal box had replaced the 1877 one in 1943. Its larger frame was required in connection with three sidings added parallel to the up refuge siding behind the engine. They served the RAF Grovely Wood Depot and were in use until about 1951. The box closed on 26th April 1982 when the 1973 barriers were automated. (Lens of Sutton)

57. Class 47 no. 1740 (later 47147) passes a mixture of ex-SR and GWR signals as it approaches the site of Wylye station with the 13.35 Bristol - Portsmouth on 27th April 1972. The old route of the A303 is in the background. (G.Gillham)

58. Viewed from the same location on 20th April 1975 we see the new bridge for the A303 in the distance and an upper quadrant arm on the GWR post. Class 9F 2-10-0 no. 92203 *Black Prince* is working a railtour from Newport in connection with a works and depot open day at Eastleigh. (A.G.Thorpe)

WEST OF WYLYE

59. The route continues west on an undulating course and passes over two accommodation crossings - Stockton and Sherrington. This is the distant signal of the former. There was a signal box at the latter location from 1914 to 1923 and from 1943 to 1953 in connection with wartime up and down loops. (H.C.Casserley)

60. A diesel railcar was recorded on a misty day in September 1936 working the 12.42pm Salisbury to Westbury, where it was due at 1.32 having called at all stations on its 24 mile journey. It had worked out from Westbury at 10.20am. (H.C.Casserley)

61. During the period from May 1966 to May 1969 when most weekday passenger turns on the Salisbury - Bath route were worked by WR diesel multiple units, there was found to be insufficient capacity for the still considerable amount of parcels and mail traffic then being carried. As a result a new daily van train ran in each direction, the eastbound working being a through service from Derby to Portsmouth via Bristol. This train was often hauled by a Midland Region class 45 Peak locomotive, as on 9th July 1968 when no. D102 (later 45140) was photographed near Sherrington, east of Codford. (G.Gillham)

CODFORD

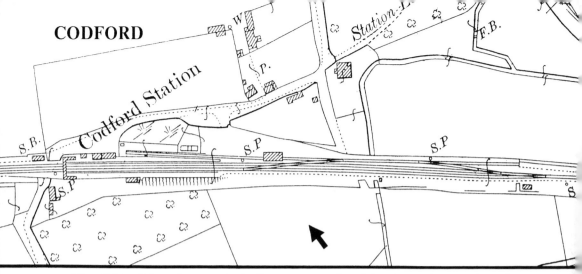

The 1901 edition shows a single line to Wylye but this had been doubled on 13th January 1900, the route to Heytesbury having been so treated in 1899. A 3-ton capacity crane was listed in 1938 whereas the other now-closed intermediate stations only had 30-cwt lifting facilities in the goods sheds.

Codford	1903	1913	1923	1933
No of passenger tickets issued	10539	10594	8758	3748
No. of season tickets issued	-	-	27	36
No. of parcels forwarded	6838	7389	16336	11584
General goods forwarded (tons)	1322	2063	1599	373
Coal, Coke etc received (tons)	487	391	149	179
Other minerals received (tons)	796	1388	719	81
General goods received (tons)	1832	1877	1277	2250
Trucks livestock forwarded	73	116	145	102

62. The signal box was opened on 5th March 1877 and a passing loop was added on 5th February 1897, together with the up platform, left. Passenger services ceased on 19th September 1955 and freight on 10th June 1963, but the down refuge siding was in place until 1968. (Lens of Sutton)

63. On the right is the 1897 down platform extension and four cattle wagons standing by the pens. In the distance, vans stand on the down refuge siding from which the Codford Camp Railway diverged during and after World War I. (Lens of Sutton)

64. The signal box worked controlled barriers from 4th April 1976 and closed on 22nd June 1982 when automatic half-barriers were installed. The village population remained between 700 and 800 but during the periods of military presence it increased greatly. (K.Robertson coll.)

65. Southern Railway stock hauled by GWR locomotives was typical of the grouping period. Bulldog class no. 3364 *Frank Bibby* was recorded near Codford on 5th July 1938. (H.C.Casserley)

66. The same locomotive was recorded entering Codford three days later with the 3.43pm Bradford -on-Avon to Portsmouth & Southsea, which called at all stations to Salisbury. The Codford Camp line had earlier diverged to the right. (H.C.Casserley)

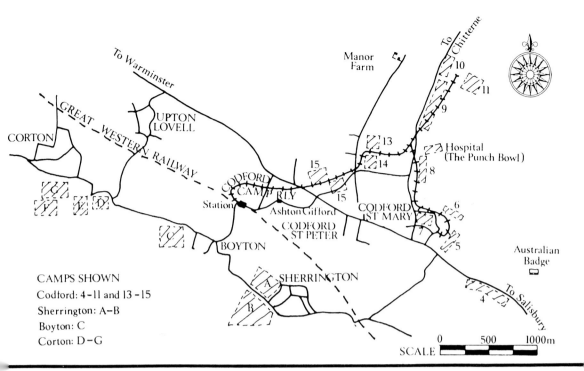

CAMPS SHOWN
Codford: 4–11 and 13–15
Sherrington: A–B
Boyton: C
Corton: D–G

SCALE 0 500 1000m

Active use of Salisbury Plain by the Army began around 1895 and was probably the stimulus for the doubling of the track. The Codford Camp Railway was in use from October 1914 until the end of 1922. (Plain Soldiering)

67. This is no. 8 Camp at Codford. The 2¾ miles of railway was worked by Avonside 0-4-0ST no. 16 *Finetta* until 1918. Thereafter the GWR provided a tank engine. (Lens of Sutton)

CAMP NO. 8. CODFORD.

68. Upton Lovell level crossing had manually operated gates until automatic half-barriers were introduced on 24th June 1982. The house was on the up side, as was a trailing siding on the other side of the road during World War I. (D.Cullum)

69. The ground frame was released from Codford box. The antiquated installation was photographed in March 1981. (D.Cullum)

HEYTESBURY

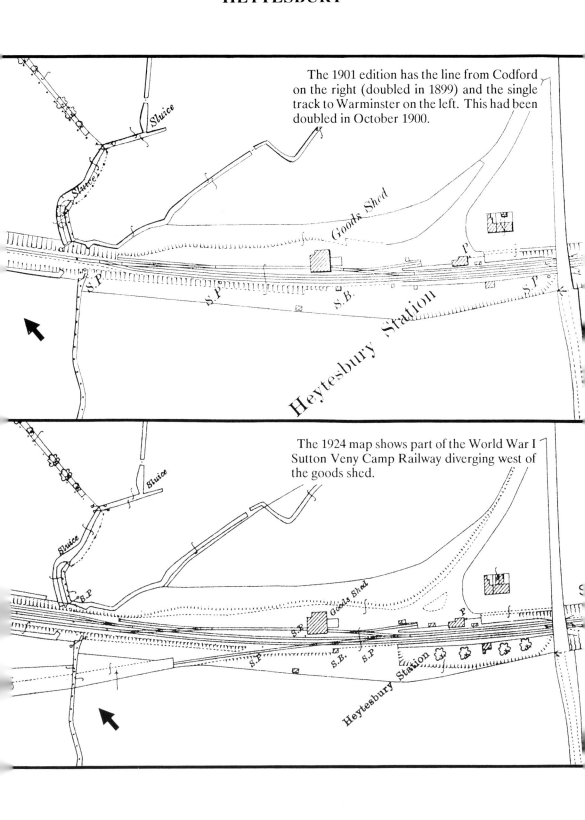

The 1901 edition has the line from Codford on the right (doubled in 1899) and the single track to Warminster on the left. This had been doubled in October 1900.

The 1924 map shows part of the World War I Sutton Veny Camp Railway diverging west of the goods shed.

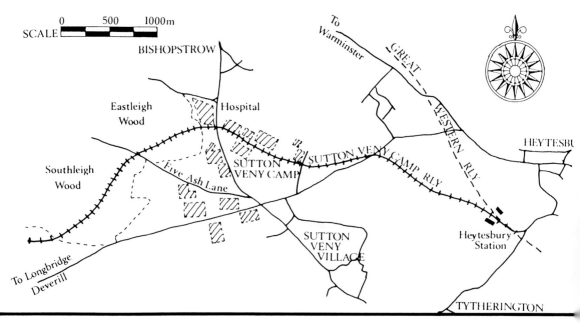

This is the approximate route of the 3½ mile long Sutton Veny Camp Railway which was lifted in about 1926. Ambulance trains were taken direct to the 1916 - built hospital operating theatre. The line was worked by Hunslet 0-6-0ST no. 38 *Jersey Marine* and Andrew Barclay 0-4-0ST *Glasgow*. (Plain Soldiering)

70. Unlike most of the other stations on the route, this one was more than half a mile from the village centre. Note the flared end on the rear coach of this up train, which is probably a family saloon. (Lens of Sutton)

71. A set of salmon pink and brown LSWR coaches and a gleeming green GWR loco- motive with glistening brasswork are about to stop at the down platform. The natural backdrop adds to the pleasurable scene. (Lens of Sutton)

72. The facilities were similar to those at the other small stations on the route but there was no footbridge. This is surprising in view of the curvature of the track causing sighting limitations. (Lens of Sutton)

ublished by
bberd Bros.,

73. This photograph is from the 1930s when there were under 450 residents locally. The figure had dropped from 1200 in 1851, the dramatic depopulation being attributed to decline in agriculture due to mechanisation and increasing food imports. Most moved to urban areas as domestic servants and rail revenue fell accordingly. (H.C.Casserley)

74. With traditional stooks and stacks in the background, class 4300 2-6-0 no. 7309 heads east with the 10.45am Bristol Temple Meads to Salisbury on 14th September 1936. All horse boxes were provided with a groom's compartment and fodder storage. (H.C.Casserley)

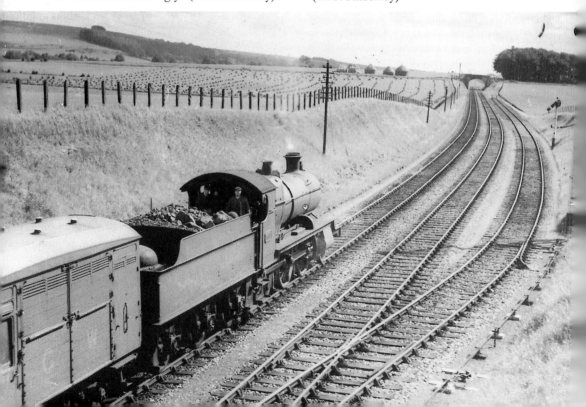

75. A change of season for this and the next photograph which date from 1st November 1937. No. 6387 of the 4300 class plods west with empty coal wagons for South Wales where they would be filled again to keep the home fires burning. The siding has its own signal post. (H.C.Casserley)

Heytesbury	1903	1913	1923	1933
No of passenger tickets issued	10908	8971	9567	1964
No. of season tickets issued	-	-	18	22
No. of parcels forwarded	10117	14253	16770	2401
General goods forwarded (tons)	904	395	1184	114
Coal, Coke etc received (tons)	1003	892	156	73
Other minerals received (tons)	438	844	634	-
General goods received (tons)	1245	819	681	360
Trucks livestock forwarded	107	173	64	27

76. One of the early members of the same class, no. 4380, passes with the 10.53am Cardiff General to Portsmouth & Southsea which ran fast between Warminster and Salisbury. This class was introduced in 1911. (H.C.Casserley)

77. Goods and passenger services were withdrawn on 19th September 1955, the down refuge siding beyond the goods shed having been lifted in 1954. To the left had been the siding to the military camp, the part on GWR property being removed in 1935.
(Lens of Sutton)

78. A view on closure day includes the Tytherington Road bridge from which many of the preceding pictures were taken. The signal box remained in use until 5th May 1968 but the up refuge siding beyond the bridge was taken out of use in December 1961.
(E.Wilmshurst)

NORTH OF HEYTESBURY

79. GWR coaches with SR class U no. 1625 graced the upper Wylye Valley on 20th July 1937 while forming the 2.37pm Portsmouth & Southsea to Cardiff General. The carriage roof boards give the train an air of importance. This locomotive was restored to work on the Mid-Hants Railway. (H.C.Casserley)

80. In the background are Scratchbury Hill and Cotley Hill which both rise to over 600 ft above sea level and add to the scenic delights of the route. No. 7804 *Baydon Manor* is passing Heytesbury down distant on 24th June 1938. (H.C.Casserley)

WARMINSTER

Almshouses

Rose Villa

G. S.P.

Station

Signal Bo

Almshouses

Stone

S.P.

F.B.

S.B.

S.P.

Post

F.B.

L.B.

W.M.

G.   W.   R.

S.P.

S.Ps

W.M.

Almshouses

S A L I S B U R Y   B R A N C H

S.P.

F.B.

S.B.

L.B.

AVENUE

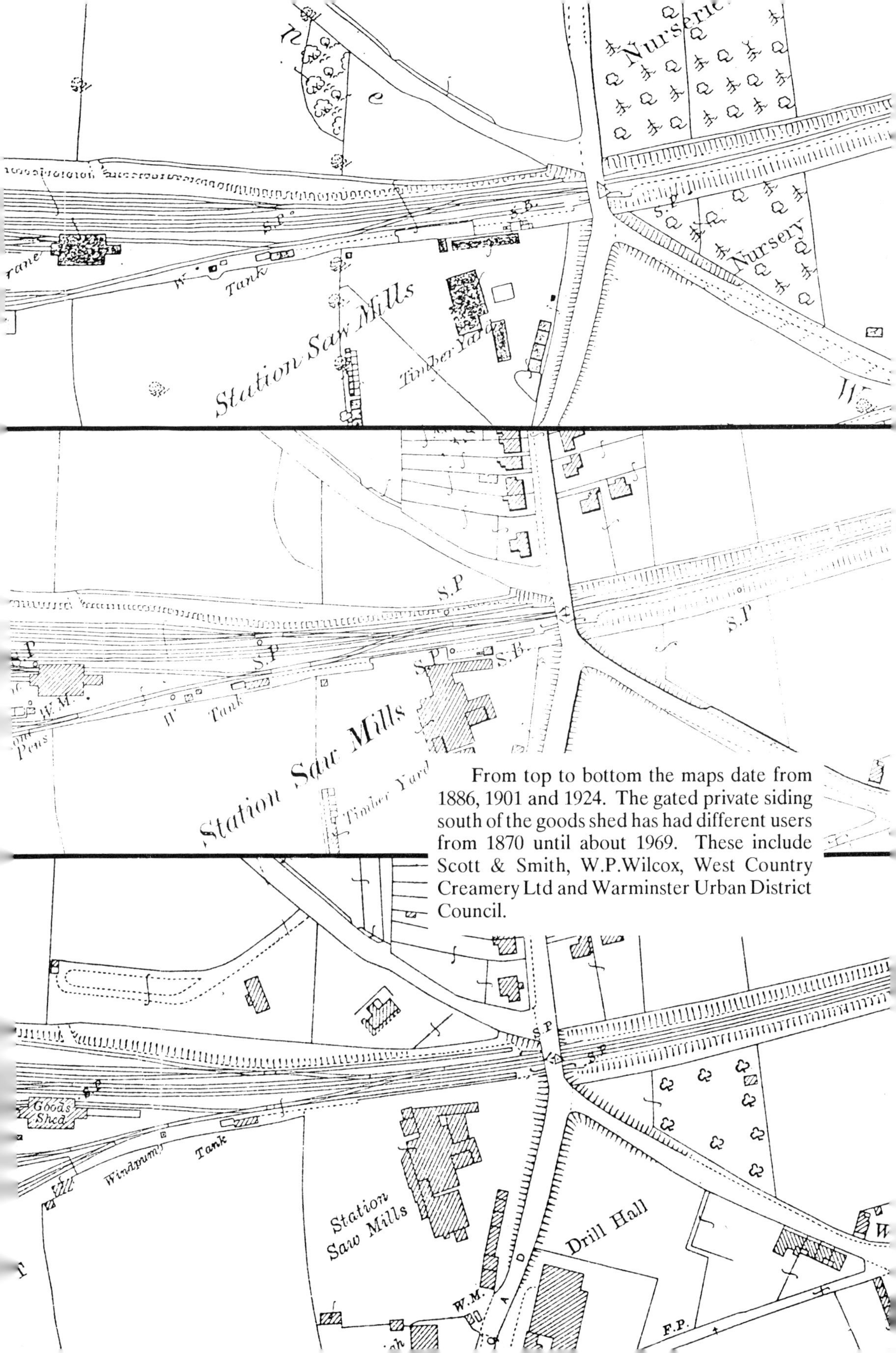

Nurserie...
Nursery

Station Saw Mills
Timber Yard
W. Tank
S.P.
S.B.
Crane

Station Saw Mills
Timber Yard
W.M.
Tank
S.P.
S.B.
Pens

From top to bottom the maps date from 1886, 1901 and 1924. The gated private siding south of the goods shed has had different users from 1870 until about 1969. These include Scott & Smith, W.P.Wilcox, West Country Creamery Ltd and Warminster Urban District Council.

Goods Shed
Windpump
Tank
Station Saw Mills
Drill Hall
W.M.
F.P.
S.P.

81. The station was a broad gauge terminus from 9th September 1851 until 30th June 1856 and is seen to retain its early overall roof in this 1928 photograph. The population of this important market and adminstrative centre was just over 6000 when the railway arrived. It increased by about 1500 in the following 100 years. (H.C.Casserley)

82. Flower class 4-4-0 no. 4172 (rebuilt Armstrong class no. 8 *Gooch*) runs in from Westbury on 29th April 1928 with GWR stock. The milk churns in this and the previous picture are a reminder of this once important traffic at this station. Ten years later the goods yard was recorded as having a 12 ton crane. (H.C.Casserley)

83. The 2.30pm from Portsmouth & Southsea to Cardiff General was hauled by U class 2-6-0 no.1624 on 21st September 1936. Notice that the old roof had been replaced by individual platform canopies by that time.
(H.C.Casserley)

Warminster	1903	1913	1923	1933
No of passenger tickets issued	47769	45070	43903	24338
No. of season tickets issued	-	-	112	328
No. of parcels forwarded	36959	60104	78940	41090
General goods forwarded (tons)	7037	7695	6939	4768
Coal, Coke etc received (tons)	8332	7457	4107	3943
Other minerals received (tons)	3742	7299	7605	2616
General goods received (tons)	15152	15327	13555	7345
Trucks livestock forwarded	318	436	607	327

84. The plain rivetted steel awning is austere when compared with the decorated valances at other stations. The footbridge roof had been removed despite this being the busiest station on the route. (C.L.Caddy)

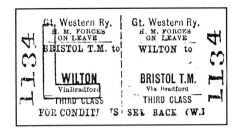

86. Class 47 no. D1736 leaves for Portsmouth on 4th September 1965. The signal box opened on 19th June 1904 and closed on 3rd June 1979, when it became a ground frame for one of the remaining two crossovers and the only siding left. These are seen in pictures 89 and 91. (C.L.Caddy)

85. The exterior was recorded in 1964 when the station was past its peak in military traffic, which was particularly heavy during and after both world wars. The Air Ministry had three sidings north of the station between 1942 and 1949. (H.C.Casserley)

87. WR Hymek class 35 diesel-hydraulics were regular performers on the Salisbury - Bath route from 1961 to 1966 and again from 1969 to 1973. Here, on 28th June 1969, no. 7009 (still in green livery but with all-yellow ends) arrives at Warminster station with the 09.50 (SO) Cardiff to Poole. The building to the extreme right was the Geest Ltd banana packing plant, served by trains of insulated vans bringing the fruit from Southampton or Bristol Docks - some empty vans can be seen in the background. The plant ceased to be rail-served in the mid-1970s and the sidings were removed during 1979. (G.Gillham)

88. The station was still gaslit in the 1960s. The GWR conveyed coal for the local gasworks until it closed in 1947, after which date gas was supplied by the Bath Gas Light Company. General freight traffic ceased on 2nd April 1973. (Lens of Sutton)

89. On 27th April 1974, no. 35028 *Clan Line* appeared on a railtour, this having been seen earlier in picture no. 45. In order to haul modern air-braked coaches, this locomotive was fitted with a compressor on the back of the tender in August 1994. (S.C.Nash)

90. The class 59s are one of the most reliable locomotives ever to run in Britain with a very high availability factor. Here no. 59003 *Yeoman Highlander* runs through the up platform on 11th September 1986 in as-new condition with a long string of empties. (D.Mitchell)

The Army and Warminster

There was considerable activity here in WWI but in WWII it was much greater with eight sidings, two loops and tank loading platforms being added at Beechgrove on the down side, one mile east of the station. A signal box was in use there from 11th April 1944 until 13th December 1949, a ground frame controlling access at other times. The RAOC depot became 1st Guards Armoured division in 1941. It was expanded in 1943 and taken over by the US Army. The REME and the School of Infantry was established here in 1945 and the Weapons Museum opened in 1970.

91. Until the arrival of the class 59s in 1986, most SR-bound stone workings required banking assistance up the 3 miles of 1 in 76/70 between Westbury and Upton Scudamore. Here, on 8th May 1987, no.56059 restarts its 2040 tonne load of PTA hoppers forming the 12.08 Whatley - Fareham away from Warminster after stopping to detach sister locomotive no.56045 (seen in background) which had been helping at the rear. (G.Gillham)

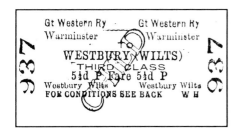

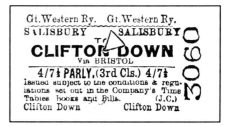

92. An autocoach with 0-6-0PT no.5421 formed the 10.45am Westbury to Warminster local service on 24th July 1937. It is near Upton Scudamore where a down trailing siding was in use from 1900 until 1964. There was also a crossover and signal box in use in that period. (H.C.Casserley)

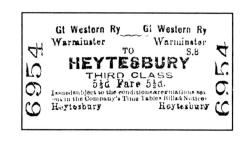

6954   Gt Western Ry   Gt Western Ry   6954
Warminster   Warminster
TO   S.8
HEYTESBURY
THIRD CLASS
5½d Fare 5½d.
Issued subject to the conditions & regulations set
out in the Company's Time Tables Bills & Notices
Heytesbury   Heytesbury

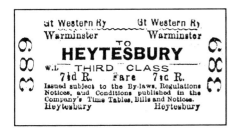

Gt Western Ry   Gt Western Ry
Warminster   Warminster
            TO
HEYTESBURY
w.L. THIRD CLASS
7½d R.   Fare   7½d R.
Issued subject to the By-laws, Regulations
Notices, and Conditions published in the
Company's Time Tables, Bills and Notices.
Heytesbury   Heytesbury

389   389

93. On 27th October 1982, the late afternoon
sun picks out no.37303 and 37299 banking a
1500 tonne Westbury - Fareham stone train up
the 1 in 70 gradient at Upton Scudamore. The
train was hauled by no.47280. (G.Gillham)

94. Roaring on full power, no.56055 raises an
Amey Roadstone train up the scarp edge of the
chalk mass of Salisbury Plain on 10th September 1987. (T. Heavyside)

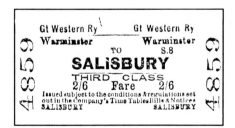

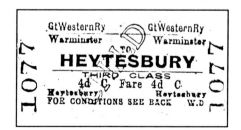

95. Some seconds later the photographer turned round to show that no.47098 was banking the rear of the train. It would be detached at Warminster and would return to Westbury. The hill is in a military training area. (T.Heavyside)

DILTON MARSH

96. The halt was opened on 1st June 1937; the platforms were staggered by 40 yds. This is the timber-built down platform in 1963, its companion being in the distance. At the end of 1969 both platforms were shortened to one coach length. (C.L.Caddy)

97. Mrs Roberts acted as a ticket agent from 1947 until at least 1969. The village had about 1500 inhabitants and so the halt had a greater potential than most of the intermediate stations. (Lens of Sutton)

98. The 10.10 from Portsmouth Harbour to Swansea speeds towards the up platform on 15th April 1988. At this period up trains called at 07.43, 08.59, 16.56 and 18.50. The waiting shelters were removed in 1991. (P.G.Barnes)

99. After several attempts to secure permanent closure, it was closed from 5th March to 30th April 1994 for complete rebuilding with metal decking at a cost of £180,000. With only a single door open on the 10.31 Bristol to Southampton train, the conductor greets two passengers. The average number here is 16 per day. (J.Scrace)

100. With the Westbury distant signal in the background, no.34037 *Clovelly* struggles up the 1 in 75 gradient with a Westbury - Poole load of cement wagons on 4th September 1965. No. D7088 is assisting at the rear. (S.C.Nash)

WESTBURY

The 1890 map at 6" to 1 mile has the line from Bath at the top, from Frome on the left and from Salisbury at the bottom. The station was nearly one mile from the centre of the old-established market town.

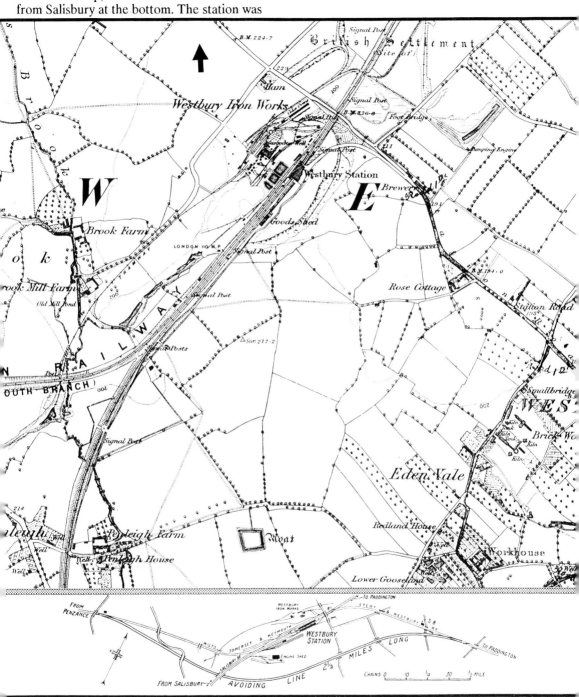

The direct line from Paddington (right) was opened in 1900. The "Avoiding Line" came into use in 1933 and avoided the speed restrictions and congestion of the station.
(Railway Magazine)

Brook Mill Farm

101. The number of platforms was doubled to four when the station was rebuilt in 1899 in readiness for the new line eastwards to Patney & Chirton which gave a more direct route to London. The staff and one symbolic milk churn were recorded on an Edwardian postcard. (Lens of Sutton)

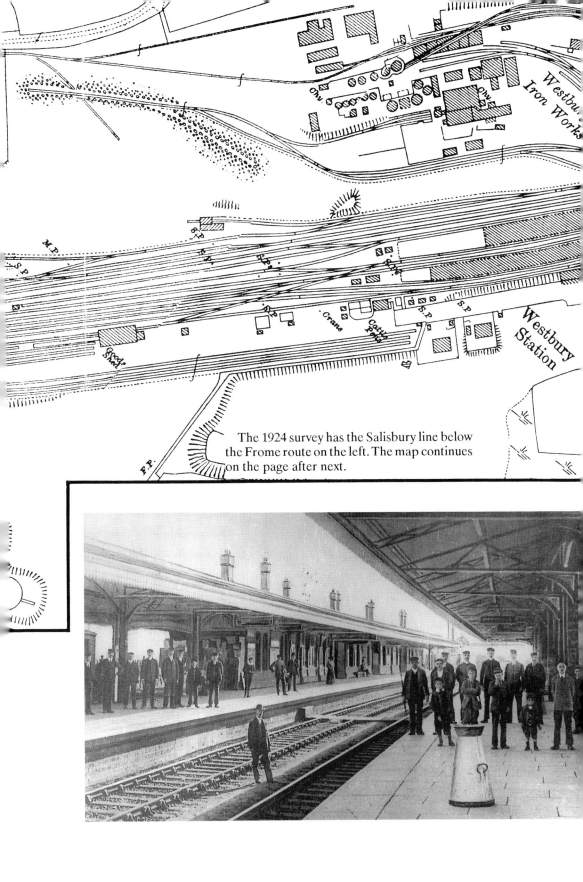

The 1924 survey has the Salisbury line below the Frome route on the left. The map continues on the page after next.

Westbury Iron Works

Westbury Station

102. A northward view in the early part of this century has Westbury Iron Works and the two pairs of main lines on the left, the station being in the distance. Beyond the right signal is Middle Box, which closed on 5th May 1968. (Lens of Sutton)

103. Looking west from the bridge approach road we cannot fail to miss the iron works but can easily not appreciate that there is an end and side loading dock between the fences. Scattered milk churns suggest one of its uses. (Lens of Sutton)

W.R. STATION
WESTBURY.

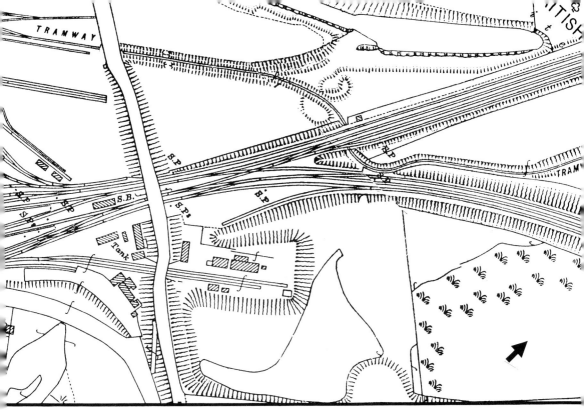

104. Westbury Iron Works had private siding facilities from 1870 to 1941. Its 1907 Peckett 0-4-0ST (works no.1099) was recorded out of use in May 1935, prior to sale in1938. Iron ore pits were situated north and south of the works, the connecting 2ft gauge tramway being shown on both maps. This had four locomotives, the first being purchased in 1874 and the last sold in February 1939. (H.C.Casserley)

105. Seen on the 1915 up goods avoiding line on 27th June 1938 is class 4300 no. 8328. There was a similar down line (opened in 1907) between North and South boxes which kept goods traffic off the four passenger lines when they were busy. Tipper wagons for iron ore are on the right. (Lens of Sutton)

106. From left to right the through lines were designated up goods, up Weymouth, up Salisbury, down Weymouth, down Salisbury and down goods. The pit was for examination of inside motion of locomotives during a journey. (Lens of Sutton)

107. Class 35 no. D7025 waits with the 10.10am Sundays only Cardiff General to Portsmouth Harbour on 2nd June 1963. The down goods line (right) was renamed down reception. Public goods traffic at this station ceased on 1st November 1966. (C.L.Caddy)

108. On a grey March day in 1972, class 42 Warship no. 812 *Royal Naval Reserve 1859-1959* passes Westbury north box with an Eastleigh-Severn Tunnel Junction class 7 fitted freight. The Warships were quite common on freight workings on this route during 1972, having been displaced from the Waterloo-Exeter passenger services in the previous October. However none of the class lasted into 1973, no. 812 being withdrawn from service on 3rd December 1972. (G.Gillham)

109. Two Hampshire 3-car sets (no.1125 leading) approach Westbury from the north working the 15.18 Bristol Temple Meads to Portsmouth Harbour on 17th September 1975. The iron works tramway once passed under the line near the rear coach. (T.Heavyside)

110. Still immaculate after its general overhaul, no.46026 *Leicestershire and Derbyshire Yeomanry* heads a train of empty stone wagons bound for Merehead Quarry past Westbury South Box on 12th September 1978. A week later saw all the semaphore signals here replaced by colour lights (worked from North Box) and the South Box demolished. (G.Gillham)

111. The new Westbury power box provides a backdrop for no. 33027 *Earl Mountbatten of Burma* as it passes with the 17.10 Cardiff to Weymouth on 4th July 1983. The box finally opened on 13th May 1984 after Westbury station had been closed for two weeks to allow the track layout to be rationalised. (G.Gillham)

112. The 08.30 Brighton to Cardiff was hauled by no. 33056 on 10th September 1987. Major remodelling in 1984 included the removal of track from platform 1 and the closure of North Box on 11th May. (T.Heavyside)

113. A May 1986 photograph shows some of the sidings used for holding stone trains to and from the Somerset quarries. The line from Salisbury descends the hill in the left background. The diesel depot is on the extreme right. (P.G.Barnes)

114. A Weymouth train leaves platform 1, the platforms having been renumbered following the alterations in May 1984. Although the trains have become shorter, their frequency has generally increased. (M.Turvey)